The SCIENCE BEHIND the ATHLETE

FORMULA ONE

India James

A Crabtree Crown Book

Crabtree Publishing
crabtreebooks.com

School-to-Home Support for Caregivers and Teachers

This appealing book is designed to teach students about core subject areas. Students will build upon what they already know about the subject, and engage in topics that they want to learn more about. Here are a few guiding questions to help readers build their comprehensions skills. Possible answers appear here in red.

Before Reading:

What do I know about Formula One?

- *I know Formula One is a sport.*
- *I know Formula One drivers race on racetracks.*

What do I want to learn about this topic?

- *I want to know when the first Formula One races were held.*
- *I want to learn how Formula One is using technology to keep the drivers safe.*

During Reading:

I'm curious to know...

- *I'm curious to know about safety features in Formula One cars.*
- *I'm curious to know how Formula One drivers train.*

How is this like something I already know?

- *I know Formula One tires are different from road tires.*
- *I know Formula One cars are made to go fast.*

After Reading:

What was the author trying to teach me?

- *The author was trying to teach me how technology is used to help keep drivers safe.*
- *The author was trying to teach me how math is used in Formula One.*

How did the photographs and captions help me understand more?

- *The photographs helped me understand how science is used in Formula One.*
- *The captions gave me extra information about the history of Formula One.*

TABLE OF CONTENTS

WHAT IS FORMULA ONE?

Formula One racecar drivers compete in some of the fastest, most advanced vehicles on the planet. Formula One racing began in 1950. Today, 20 drivers on 10 teams compete in more than 20 **grands prix** each year on five continents.

1 CARS

The first Formula One racecars went as fast as 180 miles per hour (290 km/h). It took almost four seconds to go from 0 to 60 miles per hour (97 km/h).

Today, Formula One racecars go much faster. They can reach speeds of 225 miles per hour (362 km/h). They can go from 0 to 60 miles per hour (97 km/h) in about two seconds.

HYBRID ENGINE

Today, Formula One racecars use a **hybrid** engine. This means that a **combustion engine** is paired with two **Motor Generating Units** (MGUs). These two MGUs help to turn wasted heat energy from the combustion engine into additional movement. The energy captured by these MGUs helps to power the racecar.

RACECAR SAFETY

Though racecars have gotten faster, Formula One cars must also balance this speed with safety.

FORMULA ONE FACTS

Each car is equipped with a six-point harness system for the driver. Named for the six points that connect the safety belt to the car—two shoulder straps, two leg straps, and two pelvic straps—the harness keeps the driver safe during a crash.

The area where the driver sits in the racecar is called the survival cell. It is built from carbon fiber and Kevlar, a strong material that can withstand high temperatures. This means the survival cell can absorb a hard crash while protecting the driver. It also has a fire **suppression** system. Sprays of fire-**retardant** foam can be activated by either the driver or by someone from their team.

FORMULA ONE FACTS

Along with fire suppression systems in the car, the race suit each driver wears is designed to protect them from fire for 12 seconds. The emergency response team should be able to reach any driver within this time.

A WINNING CAR

It's also important to know which car and driver won the race! Each car is equipped with **sensors** which are accurate down to the ten thousandth of a second. When races are close, this information helps determine who won.

2 TIRES

When Formula One first began, many different types of tires were used. These tires were made by five different companies. Today, each Formula One team is given the same kind of tires. The tires are all made by the same company.

RACING TIRES

Formula One tires aren't like the ones used by everyday cars on normal roads. In dry conditions, Formula One tires don't have any **treads**. These tires without treads are called slicks. They give the tire the maximum contact with the track. This means that the racecar gets as much grip as possible on the ground and can go faster.

FORMULA ONE FACTS

Racing slicks are not used when the track is wet. Tires with treads help prevent the car from sliding on water and help keep the driver safe.

There are six types of racing slicks in Formula One. Each of these has a different hardness. Soft tires help a car go faster, but they wear out quickly. Hard tires make a car go more slowly, but they last longer.

TIRE STRATEGY

Choosing which tires to use is a big part of race strategy in Formula One. Pit stops to change tires take a lot of time. Teams want to balance a fast race with few pit stops. Which tires a team uses depends on the weather, the position of a driver at the start of the race, and the condition of each racetrack.

FORMULA ONE FACTS

Red Bull Racing holds the record for the fastest pit stop in Formula One. The crew changed all four tires on Max Verstappen's racecar in 1.82 seconds at the 2019 Brazilian Grand Prix.

3 RACETRACKS

The first Formula One races took place on both public roads as well as racetracks. Though races have changed a lot since then, both types of courses are still used today.

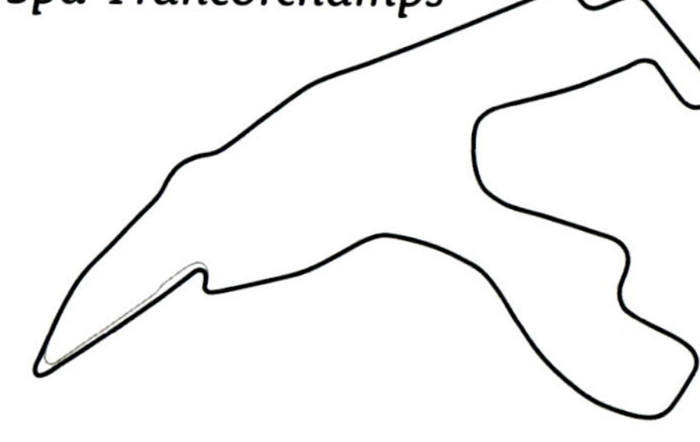

Spa-Francorchamps

FORMULA ONE FACTS

The current longest Formula One track is Spa-Francorchamps in Belgium. It is 4.352 miles (7.004 km) long.

ROAD COURSE

The Monaco Grand Prix is one of the oldest European racetracks. People were racing cars there even before Formula One was founded. The Monaco race is a road course. This means that the drivers race on public roads that are closed for the race.

FORMULA ONE FACTS

The shortest Formula One track is Monaco in Monte Carlo, Monaco. It is 2.074 miles (3.337 km) long.

Drivers at Monaco today race on a slightly different course than the first races. Many safety barriers have been added to protect both the drivers and the spectators. Different turns have been added to make the course safer and more interesting.

TRACK SAFETY

Whether new or old, tracks are always being updated for safety. Tecpro is a new type of barrier that absorbs energy better than concrete. This means that when a crash happens, the barrier crumples rather than the car. Protecting cars means that the drivers inside are protected as well.

4 TRAINING

Many of the first drivers in Formula One were older than drivers today, with their average age being 39. They also only raced part-time. Today's drivers are much younger, and racing is a full-time job.

Formula One racer and world champion Juan Manuel Fangio, 1952

Fernando Alonso of Aston Martin celebrates after the Bahrain Grand Prix of 2023 Formula One World Championship at Bahrain International Circuit.

KARTING

The best Formula One drivers begin racing when they are kids. Most drivers start out in **karting**. Drivers can participate in these races when they are as young as five years old. Karting can provide skills that are needed to become a racecar driver.

WORKOUTS

Formula One drivers are athletes. They use strength training to target specific muscle groups. Cardio workouts help increase their endurance.

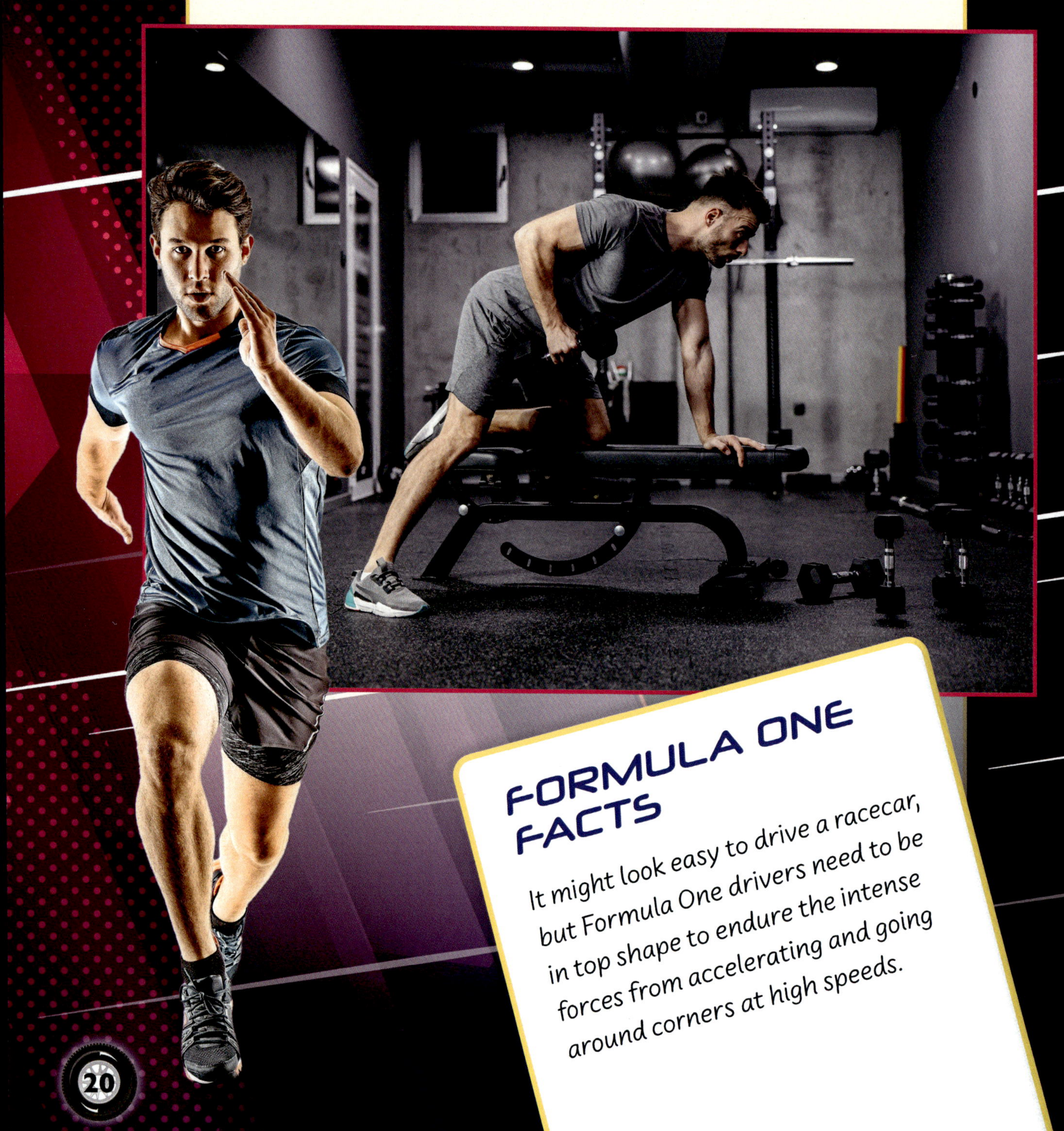

FORMULA ONE FACTS

It might look easy to drive a racecar, but Formula One drivers need to be in top shape to endure the intense forces from accelerating and going around corners at high speeds.

REFLEXES

Drivers also need to make split-second decisions and react to what happens on the track. They train to improve their reflexes and reaction time. The BlazePod system is a game of flashing lights. Drivers try to touch a flashing light as fast as possible. This helps drivers improve their reaction time.

FORMULA ONE FACTS

Formula One isn't the only sport to train for reaction times. Football, tennis, basketball, and other types of car racing all use systems like BlazePod to help their athletes prepare for a game or match.

SIMULATORS

Formula One drivers train for each racetrack by practicing in simulators. These simulators are a lot like a video game: video displays show what the driver will see on each track, and the drivers practice driving in the race by sitting in a replica of their racecar. The drivers try to make their practice as much like the race as possible. They even wear the clothes they'll wear on race days. This practice helps the drivers plan for what the race will be like.

FORMULA ONE FACTS

Many drivers have simulators at home as well as at their team's headquarters. Home simulators are not as complex, but they let the driver practice more often.

5 STATISTICS

High speed and close passes might be the most exciting parts of the race, but Formula One is a sport that depends heavily on math. **Statistics** is one area where math is used to help understand the sport.

STATISTICS

Statistics is an area of math that collects, organizes, and **analyzes** sets of numbers. In Formula One, statistics are used to explain how drivers are performing and how cars are racing. **Engineers**, drivers, and the media all use statistics to understand how cars and teams are performing.

DRIVER STATISTICS

It’s important to know how racecar drivers are performing so that coaches and engineers can help them improve. Statistics such as the number of races a driver has won and the number of points they have earned in a season help describe a driver's performance.

Lewis Hamilton's Formula One Statistics

Season	Series	Team	Races	Wins	Poles	F/Laps	Podiums	Points	Position
2007	Formula One	Vodafone McLaren Mercedes	17	4	6	2	12	109	**2nd**
2008	Formula One	Vodafone McLaren Mercedes	18	5	7	1	10	98	**1st**
2009	Formula One	Vodafone McLaren Mercedes	17	2	4	0	5	49	5th
2010	Formula One	Vodafone McLaren Mercedes	19	3	1	5	9	240	4th
2011	Formula One	Vodafone McLaren Mercedes	19	3	1	3	6	227	5th
2012	Formula One	Vodafone McLaren Mercedes	20	4	7	1	7	190	4th
2013	Formula One	Mercedes-AMG Petronas F1 Team	19	1	5	1	5	189	4th
2014	Formula One	Mercedes-AMG Petronas F1 Team	19	11	7	7	16	384	**1st**
2015	Formula One	Mercedes-AMG Petronas F1 Team	19	10	11	8	17	381	**1st**
2016	Formula One	Mercedes-AMG Petronas F1 Team	21	10	12	3	17	380	**2nd**
2017	Formula One	Mercedes-AMG Petronas Motorsport	20	9	11	7	13	363	**1st**
2018	Formula One	Mercedes-AMG Petronas Motorsport	21	11	11	3	17	408	**1st**
2019	Formula One	Mercedes-AMG Petronas Motorsport	21	11	5	6	17	413	**1st**
2020	Formula One	Mercedes-AMG Petronas F1 Team	16	11	10	6	14	347	**1st**
2021	Formula One	Mercedes-AMG Petronas F1 Team	22	8	5	6	17	387.5	**2nd**
2022	Formula One	Mercedes-AMG Petronas F1 Team	22	0	0	2	9	240	6th
2023	Formula One	Mercedes-AMG Petronas F1 Team	1	0	0	0	0	10	5th

FORMULA ONE FACTS

Lewis Hamilton has won the most Formula One races. As of 2022, he has had 103 wins.

CAR STATISTICS

Formula One racecars have hundreds of sensors. These sensors collect important information about how the car is working. Engineers can use this information to solve car problems even while the race is taking place.

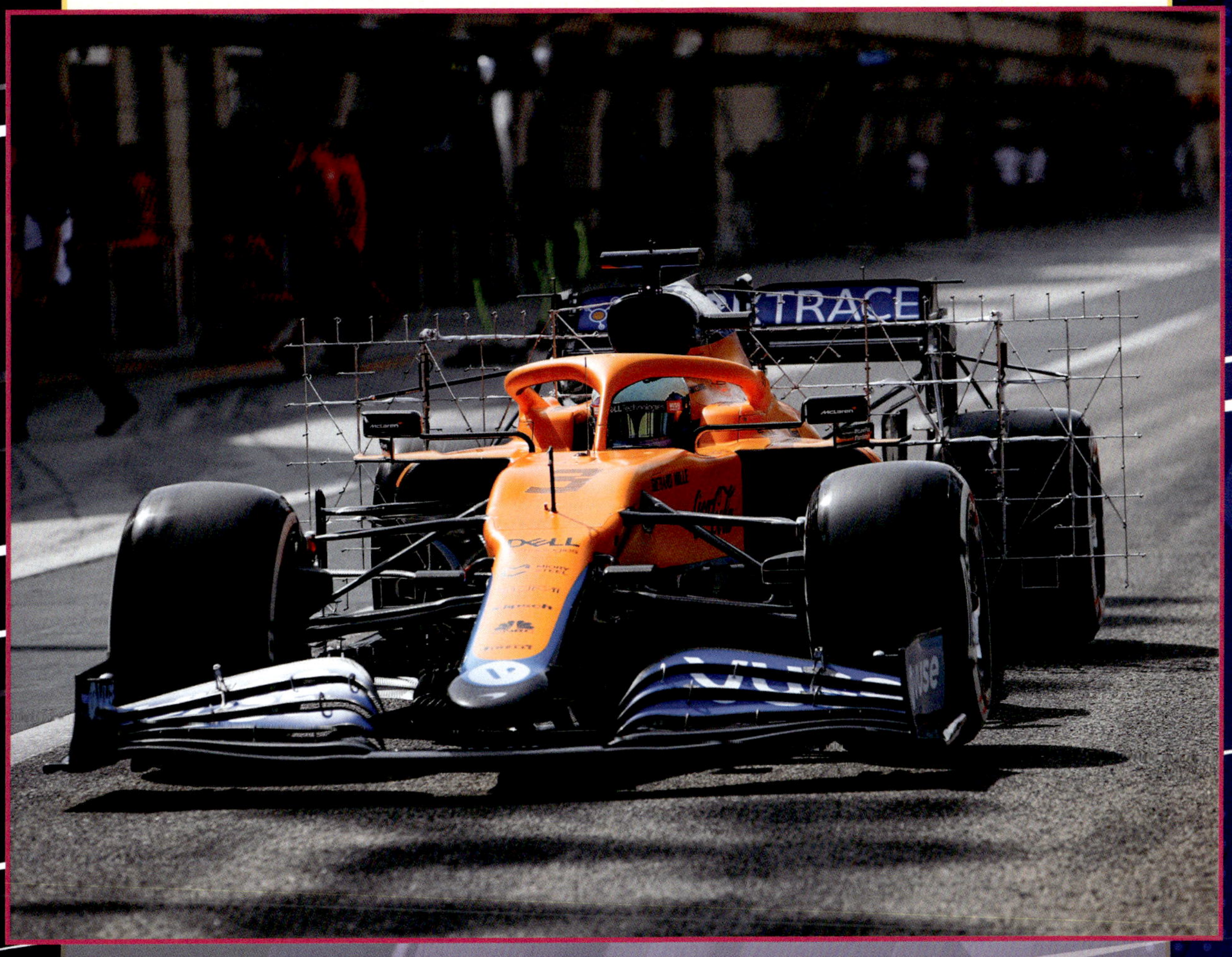

Sensors are found in various places throughout a Formula One racecar. Most of them are small and not visible from the outside.

Engineers use the sensors to measure how fast the car uses fuel. They can also see information such as brake performance. If things don't look right, engineers can tell a driver to pull into the pit lane so the car can be fixed.

CONCLUSION

Drivers in Formula One race some of the fastest cars. The cars, racetrack safety features, and training have changed since the early days of car racing. Science and technology can help make the sport faster and safer in the future.

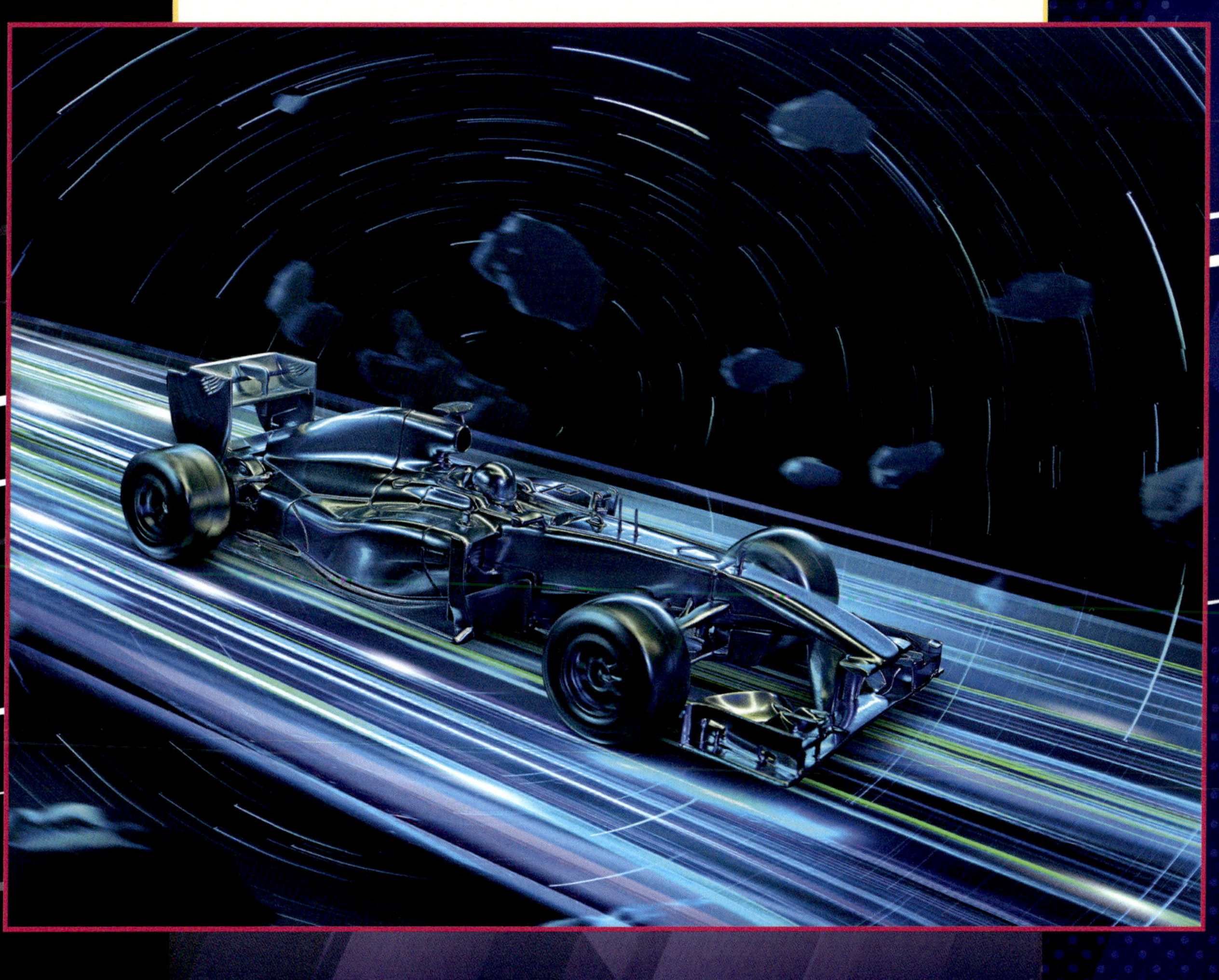

GLOSSARY

analyze (AN-uh-lize): To examine carefully and in detail

combustion engine (kuhm-BUHS-chun EN-jun): An engine that converts energy from the heat of burning gasoline into motion

engineer (en-juh-NEER): A person who is trained in the use of math, science, and creative thinking to design things that solve problems and meet needs

grands prix (grahn PREEZ): The name for Formula One races

hybrid (HAHY-brid): Something that is formed by combining two or more things together

karting (KAHRT-ing): The sport of racing small, open, four-wheeled vehicles

motor generating unit (MOH-ter JEN-uh-reyt-ing YOO-nit): Part of a racecar's engine that helps turn wasted heat energy from the combustion engine into additional movement

retardant (ri-TAHR-dnt): Something that is able to slow down the progress of something

sensor (SEN-ser): An electronic device that measures and monitors conditions from its environment

statistics (stuh-TIS-tiks): A branch of math that collects, organizes, and analyzes numbers

suppression (su-PRESH-un): Something that prevents or controls something

tread (tred): The pattern of raised lines on a tire's surface

INDEX

COMPREHENSION QUESTIONS

1. When did Formula One racing begin?
   a. 1900
   b. 1950
   c. 1976

2. How many companies make Formula One tires today?
   a. one
   b. five
   c. three

3. What is an example of a statistic measured in Formula One?
   a. driver jump height
   b. timed 100-yard dash
   c. number of races won

4. True or False: Math is important in Formula One.

5. True or False: Formula One racecars used to be faster than they are today.

Answers: 1. B, 2. A, 3. C, 4. True, 5. False

ABOUT THE AUTHOR

India James writes about science, technology, and math for young readers. She loves when science comes together with sports. India lives in Ohio with her family.

Written by: India James
Designed by: Kathy Walsh
Series Development: James Earley
Proofreader: Melissa Boyce
Educational Consultant: Marie Lemke M.Ed.

Photographs: Shutterstock; Cover & Title pg: motorsports Photographer , Lilo Alfonso, geen graphy, your; p 2-31 backgrounds: Lilo Alfonso, your; pg numbers: Tomacco; p 4: Ev. Safronov; p 5: Bob Cullinan; p 6: Jay Hirano Photography; p 7: ZRyzner; p 8: Cineberg, XpbviaNewscom; p 9: A3397 Gero BreloerviaNewscom; p 10: Piotr Piatrouski; p 11: Zryzner, Hoch Zwei; p 12: Lorenza Marzocchi, Hoch ZweiviaNewscom; p 13: XpbviaNewscom; p 14: @Wiki, grebeshkovmaxim; p 15: cristiqno barni, Alex Tihonovs; p 16 & 17: cristiano barni p 18: Beata Zawrzelvia Newscom, @Wiki; p 19: Volodymyr Gatsura; p 20: Dusan Petkovic, OSTILL is Franck Camhi; p 21: Jacob Lund; p 22: Enfoca y dispara, p 23: Ancapital; p 24: DppiviaNewscom; p 25: Jordan Tan; p 26: cristiano barni, @Wiki; p 27: Dppi/Florent Goodenvia Newscom; p 28: Dppi/DLPsviaNewscom; p 29: Doitforfun

Crabtree Publishing

crabtreebooks.com 800-387-7650

Printed in Canada/012024/CP20231127

Published in Canada
Crabtree Publishing
616 Welland Ave.
St. Catharines, Ontario
L2M 5V6

Published in the United States
Crabtree Publishing
347 Fifth Ave
Suite 1402-145
New York, NY 10016

Library and Archives Canada Cataloguing in Publication
Available at Library and Archives Canada

Library of Congress Cataloging-in-Publication Data
Available at the Library of Congress

Hardcover: 978-1-0398-3898-7
Paperback: 978-1-0398-3983-0
Ebook (pdf): 978-1-0398-4057-7
Epub: 978-1-0398-4129-1